The Big Question™

Why do most athelets fail?

Published by Adventurous Publishing
Copyright © 2024 David Hobson

Paperback ISBN: 978-1-915862-52-5
Hardback ISBN: 978-1-915862-53-2

Welcome to this edition on

Sports

Ft David Hobson

Co - Founder - PFSA

Contents

OUR
WHY

The Big Question is a brand that delve's deep into the minds of influential leaders and uncover their strategies through asking Big questions.

We believe that the journey from aspiration to achievement is both fascinating and instructive.

By asking leaders profound questions about their experiences, we gain valuable insights that can guide you in turning your own dreams into tangible outcomes.

In this book, we speak to David Hobson, legendary football scout and co-founders of the PFSA, on why most athletes fail.

Best,

-TBQ

Introduction

My name is David Hobson, and I've spent nearly three decades in football scouting, working with top clubs like Blackburn Rovers, Bolton Wanderers, and Manchester United.

Over the years, I've witnessed countless young athletes with immense potential, yet only a few manage to reach the pinnacle of success.

This book delves into why that happens, drawing from my personal experiences and lessons learned in the world of football scouting.

Chapter one

A scouts beginning

My journey into football scouting started unexpectedly in the mid-nineties.

It all began with a casual conversation with a man named Bill Hurst, a scout who had been watching my son play football.

After weeks of seeing him on the sidelines, I decided to give him a call, asking if he'd be attending another match. To my surprise, Bill had decided to quit scouting, handing over the job to a policeman. On a whim, I mentioned that I wouldn't mind doing something like that myself. Bill told me that if the new scout didn't work out, he'd let me know.

I didn't think much of it at the time. Scouting seemed like a world far removed from my everyday life. But, three months later, I received a call from Bill.

The policeman had given up on the job, and Bill asked if I was still interested. The next day, I found myself heading to Blackburn Rovers' training ground, marking the start of my unexpected career in professional football scouting.

My first experience as a scout with Blackburn Rovers was both thrilling and sobering. I was excited to be involved in professional football, but I quickly realized that the reality of scouting was far different from what I had imagined. I recommended a player, Alex Taylor, who eventually became a head coach at Blackpool Football Club.

However, the communication from the club was poor, and I often found out that players I had suggested were signed without my knowledge.

This lack of communication and acknowledgement began to wear on me. I had envisioned a close-knit relationship with the club, where my insights would be valued and acted upon. Instead, I felt like a small, unnoticed cog in a vast machine.

Disillusioned, I spoke to Bill about my frustrations. He suggested that perhaps it was time to consider moving to another club.

Not long after, I made the transition to Bolton Wanderers, another Premier League club at the time.

Bolton was a completely different experience. I was given more responsibility, overseeing an area with several scouts under my supervision. I enjoyed the challenge and the autonomy, but it wasn't without its own set of frustrations.

One particular incident stands out. I recommended a player from a small amateur club in the North West counties to the new head of recruitment. I knew this kid had potential. However, after watching him play, the feedback I received was dismissive; they thought the player was "rubbish."

That player's name was Matty Derbyshire, and just a few weeks later, Blackburn Rovers signed him. Matty went on to play for Blackburn's first team and eventually for England.

As I established myself at Bolton, Manchester United eventually came knocking. They offered me a position, but I turned them down—twice. I was content at Bolton, where I had a good working relationship with the club and was happy with how things were progressing.

However, changes at Bolton, including the arrival of a new head of recruitment who didn't appreciate my methods, led me to reconsider. Eventually, I accepted Manchester United's offer.

Chapter two

Oh united

Joining Manchester United was a significant milestone in my career. For 13 years, I worked at one of the biggest clubs in the world, identifying talent and advocating for the potential I saw in young players.

However, even at a club as prestigious as Manchester United, I faced many of the same challenges I had encountered at Blackburn and Bolton. Ultimately, decisions about which players to sign lay with the club's higher-ups, and often, my recommendations were not acted upon.

One particularly memorable case was Jadon Sancho. I spotted him when he was just 14 and recommended him to Manchester United. At the time, the club wasn't interested, focusing on other players instead.

Years later, United bought him for £83 million.

Chapter Three

The problem

In 2012, the landscape of football scouting changed dramatically with the introduction of the Elite Player Performance Plan (EPPP) by the FA. This new plan required all scouts to have a formal qualification.

The problem was that no such qualification existed. Instead of seeing this as a setback, I saw an opportunity. If no one else was going to create a course, then I would.

I spent time researching and developing the first-ever course in talent identification and development. My first students were scouts from Manchester United and Manchester City—a unique gathering that will likely never happen again.

The course was a success, and soon I was conducting sessions not just in England but internationally, in places like Egypt, the United States, and Scotland.

As I developed the course and taught it to aspiring scouts, I realized that education and discipline are often overlooked factors in an athlete's success. It's not just about being able to kick a ball well. For young athletes, having a strong foundation in education is crucial.

I've seen countless talented players who failed to make it because they didn't possess the discipline or the academic skills needed to navigate the complexities of a professional career.

Take math and English, for example. These subjects might not seem directly related to football, but they play a critical role in a player's development. Math helps with spatial awareness, timing, and understanding strategy, while English is essential for communication, both on and off the pitch.

Players who lack these skills often struggle to adapt to the professional environment, where understanding contracts, managing finances, and communicating effectively are just as important as playing the game.

Chapter Four

New beginnings

The scouting course didn't just teach the technical aspects of talent identification; it opened doors for many individuals who might not have had the opportunity otherwise.

Former players, aspiring scouts, and even those with no prior football experience were given the tools they needed to break into the industry. Over time, the FA and Scottish FA developed their own courses, but by then, I had already made my mark.

One of my proudest achievements is the Women's Football Scouting and Analysis Course, which we launched recently. It's the first of its kind, and I believe it will open doors for many women who want to work in football.

The success of these courses has shown that education and structured training can significantly impact not just the scouts, but the athletes they work with as well.

So, why do most athletes fail? Through my experiences, I've learned that it's rarely due to a lack of talent. More often, it's about timing, opportunity, and the ability to navigate the complex world of professional sports.

Athletes fail because the right people don't see them at the right time, because they don't have the support they need to develop, or simply because the subjective nature of scouting overlooks their potential.

Education and discipline play a critical role in this equation. Many young athletes lack the academic foundation or the personal discipline required to succeed at the highest levels. Football, like life, is full of stories of near misses—of talents that went unrecognized, and of players who were told they weren't good enough only to prove everyone wrong.

My journey in football has been about more than just finding the next big star; it's been about understanding why so many players, despite their potential, don't make it. And the answer, as I've discovered, is as complex as the game itself.

My big question to you is..

What makes you stand out?

About the author

David Hobson is a co-founder of the PFSA with over 20 years experience of scouting for Manchester United, Bolton and Blackburn.

David used to be a coordinator for one of United's development centres in the north west of England.

Be you,
be bold,
Go big.

-TBQ

Notes

THE B!G QUESTION.

_____
_____
_____
_____
_____
_____
_____
_____
_____
_____
_____
_____
_____
_____
_____
_____
_____
_____.............Go big

THE B!G QUESTION.

_____

_____

_____

_____

_____

_____

_____

_____

_____

_____

_____

_____

_____

_____

_____

_____..............Go big

THE B!G QUESTION.

_____

_____

_____

_____

_____

_____

_____

_____

_____

_____

_____

_____

_____

_____

_____..............Go big

THE B!G QUESTION.

_____

_____

_____

_____

_____

_____

_____

_____

_____

_____

_____

_____

_____

_____

_____

_____..............Go big

THE B!G QUESTION.

_____

_____

_____

_____

_____

_____

_____

_____

_____

_____

_____

_____

_____

_____

_____

_____..............Go big

THE B!G QUESTION.

_____
_____
_____
_____
_____
_____
_____
_____
_____
_____
_____
_____
_____
_____
_____
_____..............Go big

THE B!G QUESTION.

_____
_____
_____
_____
_____
_____
_____
_____
_____
_____
_____
_____
_____
_____
_____
_____
...............Go big

THE B!G QUESTION.

_____

_____

_____

_____

_____

_____

_____

_____

_____

_____

_____

_____

_____

_____

...............Go big

THE B!G QUESTION.

_____
_____
_____
_____
_____
_____
_____
_____
_____
_____
_____
_____
_____
_____
_____
_____
_____..............Go big

THE B!G QUESTION.

_____
_____
_____
_____
_____
_____
_____
_____
_____
_____
_____
_____
_____
_____
_____
_____
_____ ....GO B!G

THE B!G QUESTION.

_____
_____
_____
_____
_____
_____
_____
_____
_____
_____
_____
_____
_____
_____
_____..............GO B!G

THE B!G QUESTION.

_____
_____
_____
_____
_____
_____
_____
_____
_____
_____
_____
_____
_____
_____
_____
_____
_____
............GO B!G
_____

THE B!G QUESTION.

..............GO B!G

THE B!G QUESTION.

_____
_____
_____
_____
_____
_____
_____
_____
_____
_____
_____
_____
_____
_____
_____
_____
_____
_____..............GO B!G

THE B!G QUESTION.

_____

_____

_____

_____

_____

_____

_____

_____

_____

_____

_____

_____

_____

_____

_____

_____

............GO B!G

THE B!G QUESTION.

_____
_____
_____
_____
_____
_____
_____
_____
_____
_____
_____
_____
_____
_____
_____
_____..............GO B!G

THE B!G QUESTION.

_____
_____
_____
_____
_____
_____
_____
_____
_____
_____
_____
_____
_____
_____
_____
.............GO B!G

THE B!G QUESTION.

_____
_____
_____
_____
_____
_____
_____
_____
_____
_____
_____
_____
_____
_____
_____
_____
_____
_____
_____
................GO B!G

THE B!G QUESTION.

_____

_____

_____

_____

_____

_____

_____

_____

_____

_____

_____

_____

_____

_____

_____

_____

_____

_____

_____

_____..........GO B!G

THE B!G QUESTION.

_____
_____
_____
_____
_____
_____
_____
_____
_____
_____
_____
_____
_____
_____
_____
_____
_____...........GO B!G

THE B!G QUESTION.

_____

_____

_____

_____

_____

_____

_____

_____

_____

_____

_____

_____

_____

_____

_____

_____

_____..........GO B!G

THE B!G QUESTION.

_____
_____
_____
_____
_____
_____
_____
_____
_____
_____
_____
_____
_____
_____
_____
_____...........GO B!G

THE B!G QUESTION.

.............GO B!G

THE B!G QUESTION.

_____
_____
_____
_____
_____
_____
_____
_____
_____
_____
_____
_____
_____
_____
_____
_____
_____............GO B!G

THE B!G QUESTION.

_____
_____
_____
_____
_____
_____
_____
_____
_____
_____
_____
_____
_____
_____
_____
_____
_____
_____
_____..........GO B!G

THE B!G QUESTION.

_____
_____
_____
_____
_____
_____
_____
_____
_____
_____
_____
_____
_____
_____
_____
_____
_____............GO B!G

THE B!G QUESTION.

_____

_____

_____

_____

_____

_____

_____

_____

_____

_____

_____

_____

_____

_____

_____

_____

_____

_____

_____

............GO B!G

THE B!G QUESTION.

_____
_____
_____
_____
_____
_____
_____
_____
_____
_____
_____
_____
_____
_____
_____
_____...........GO B!G

in The Big Question

⊙ @thebigquestionhq

✉ thebigquestioninfo@gmail.com

" GO B!G...

www.ingramcontent.com/pod-product-compliance
Lightning Source LLC
LaVergne TN
LVHW022013080426
835513LV00009B/692